I0413657

Monkey Coloring Book For Adults

Monkey Coloring Book, Advanced Adult Coloring Books for Stress Relief and Relaxation

Realistic Animals Coloring Book: Vol 11

by Amanda Davenport

Copyright © 2016 by Amanda Davenport
All rights reserved. No part of this publication may be reproduced, distributed, or transmitted in any form or by any means, including photocopying, recording, or other electronic or mechanical methods, without the prior written permission of the publisher.

ISBN-13: 978-1533468857

ISBN-10: 1533468850

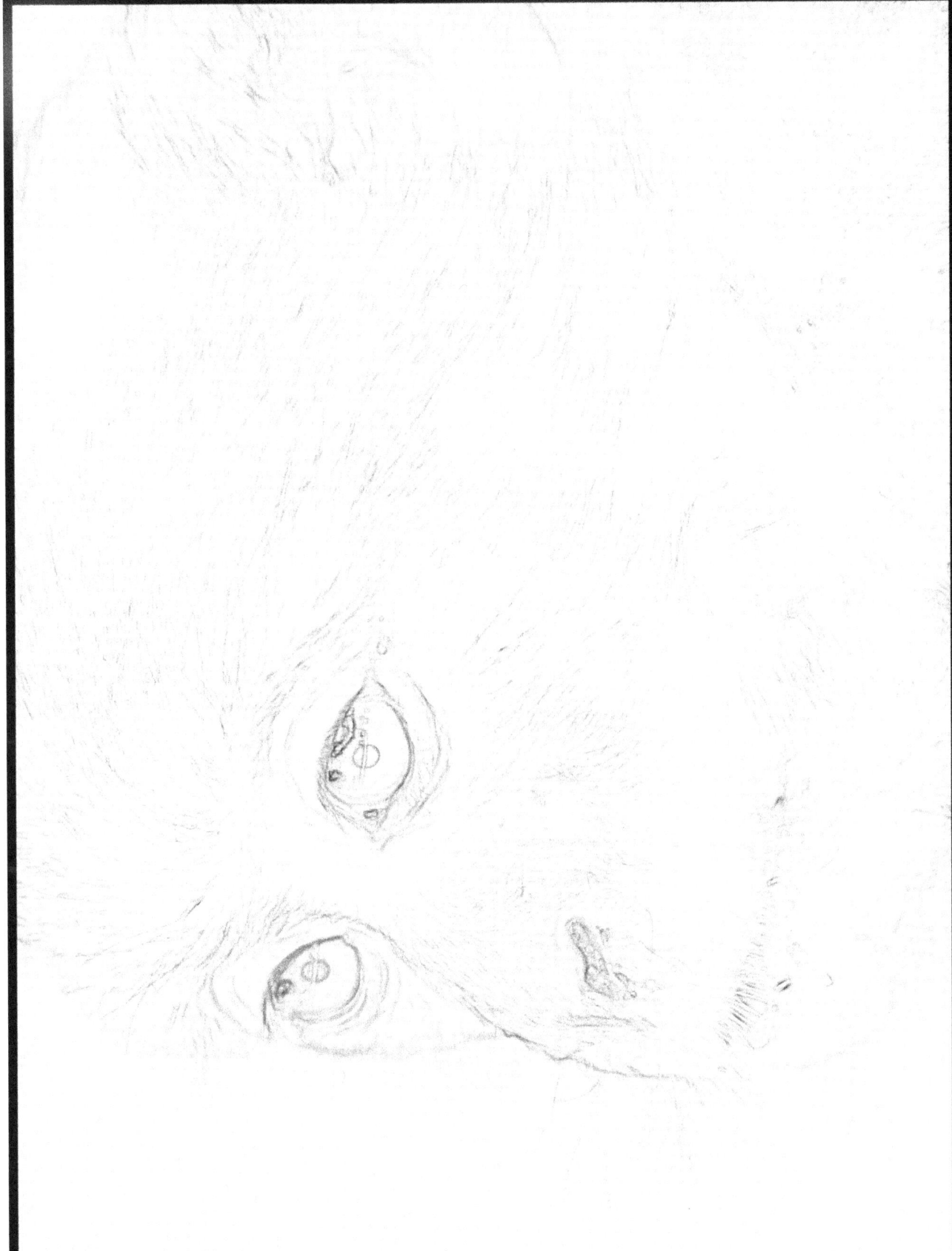

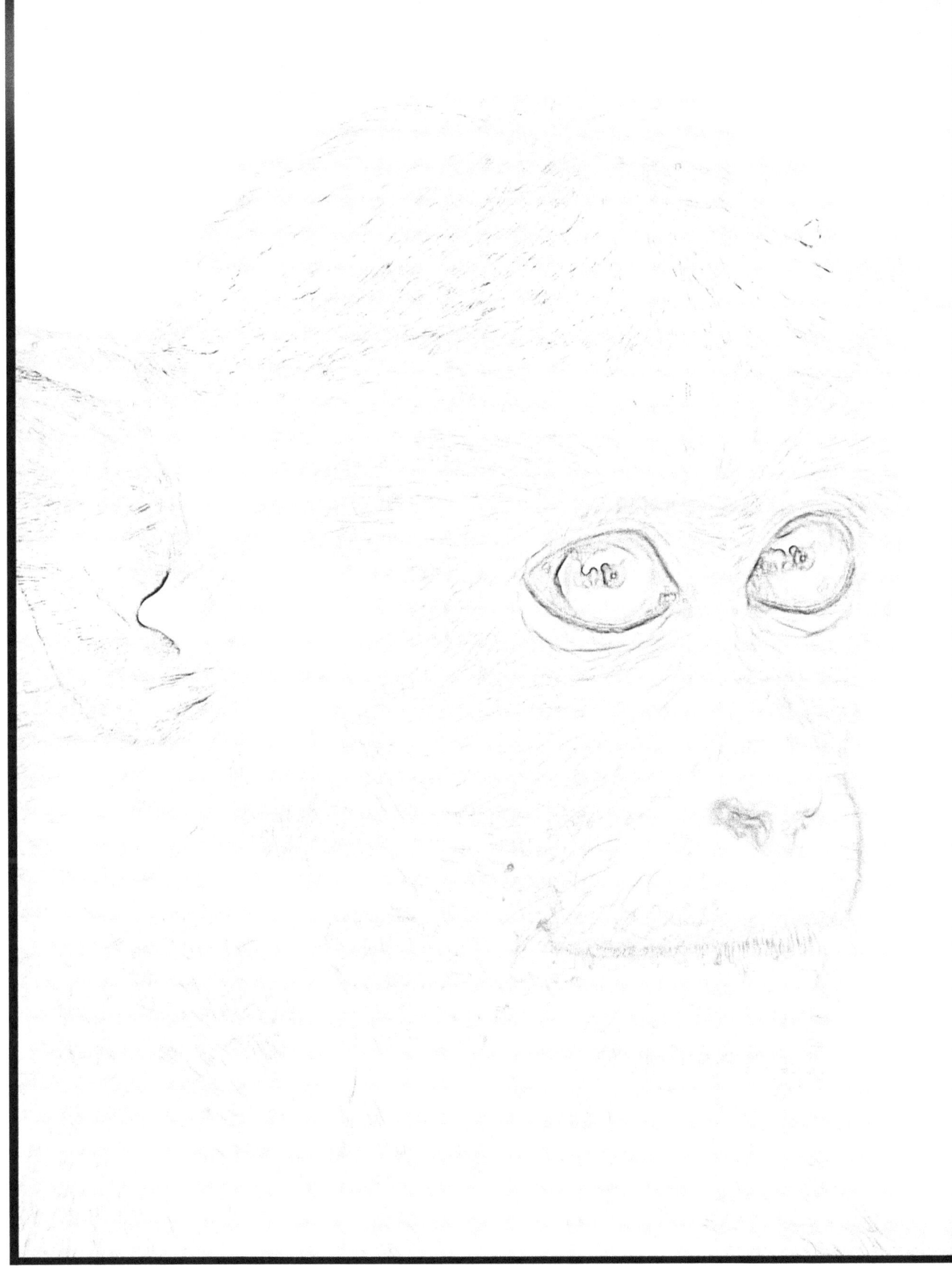

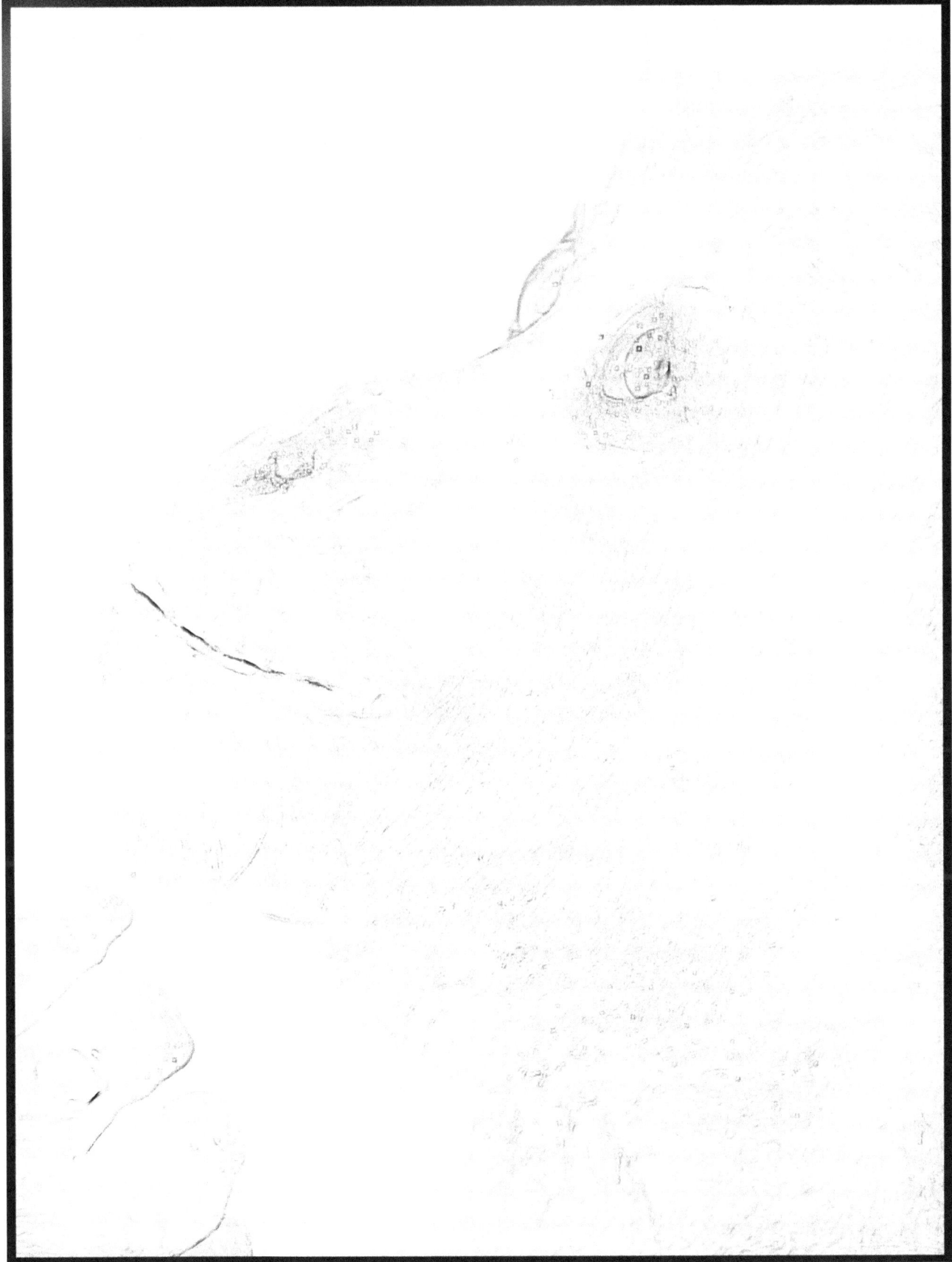

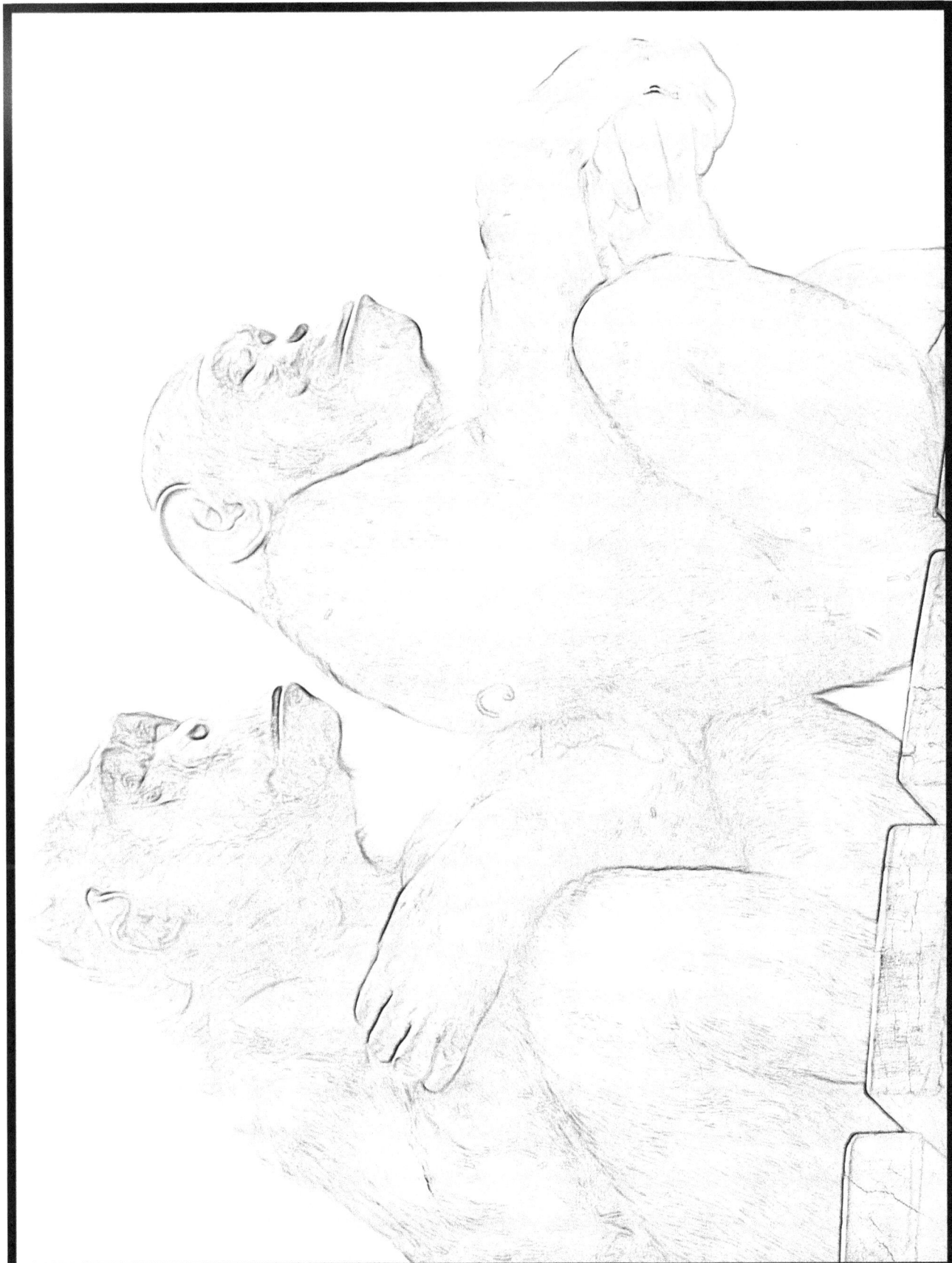

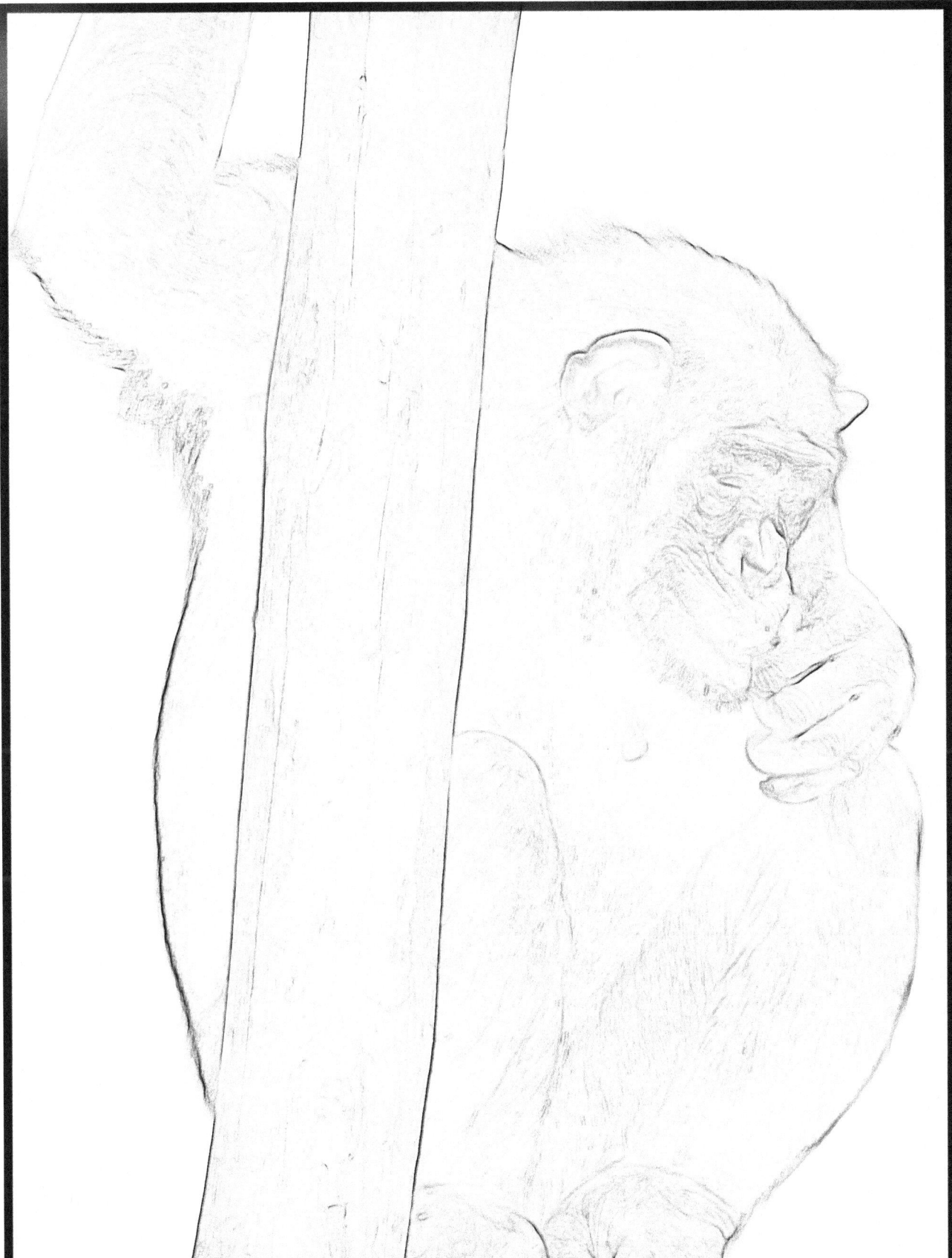

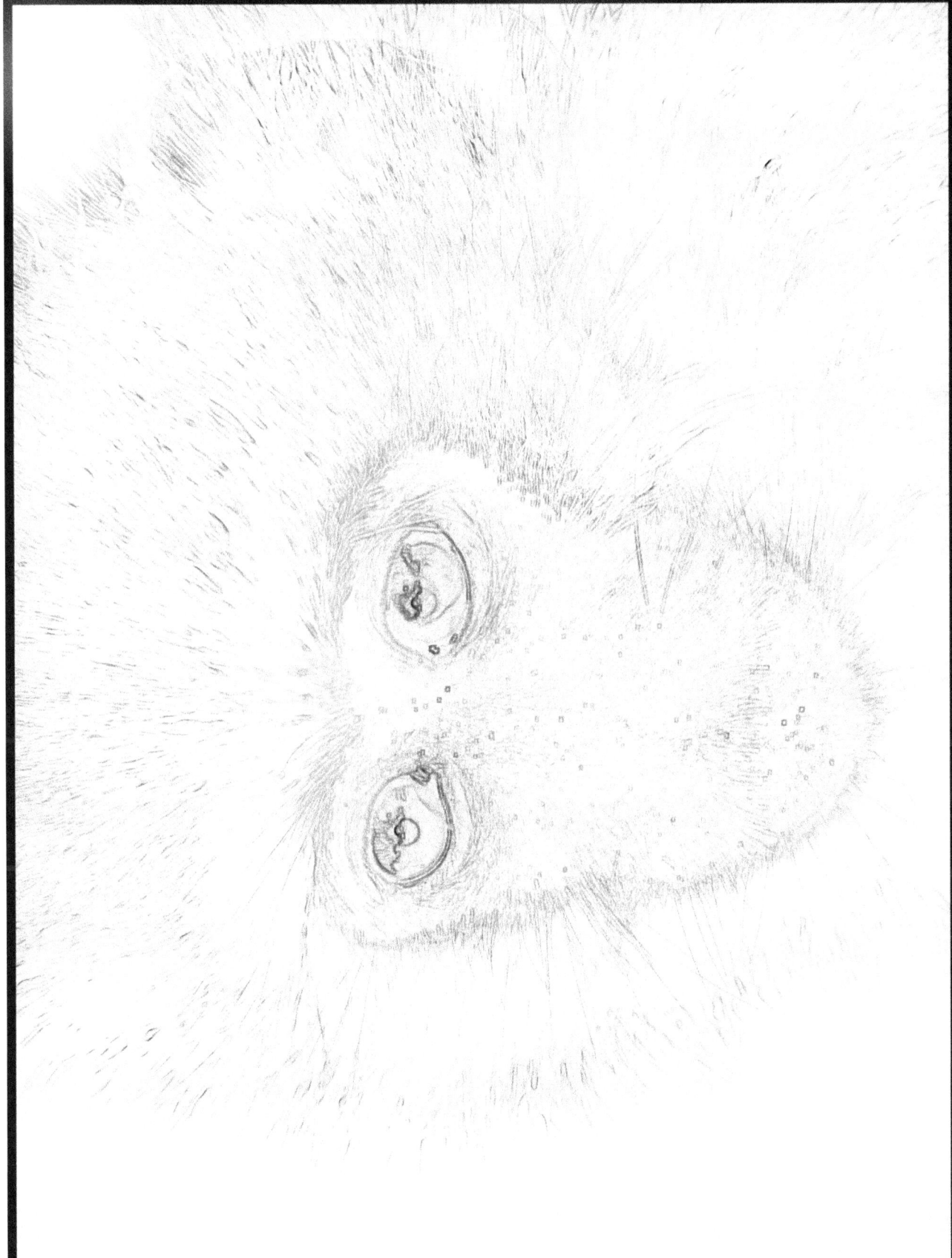

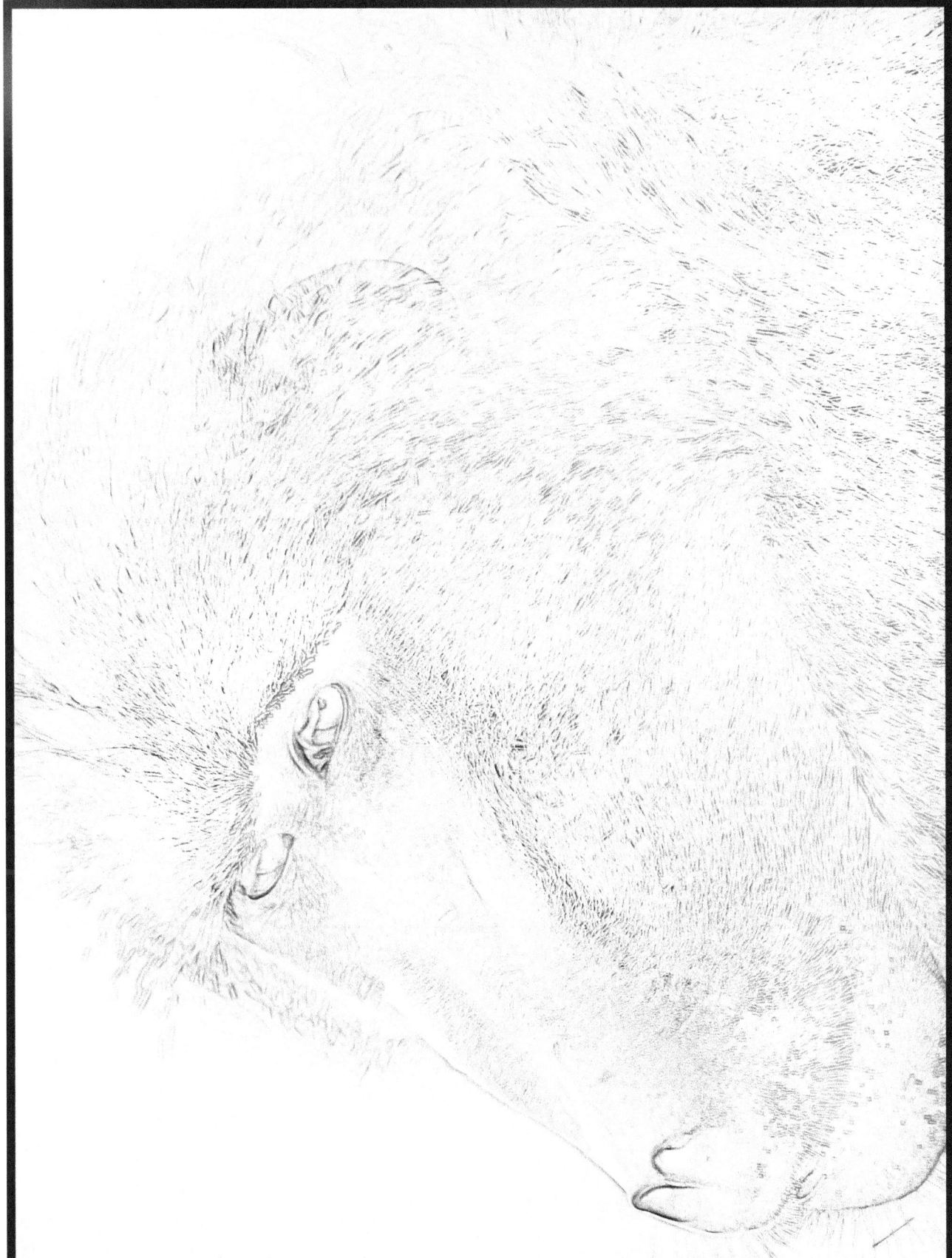

COLOR TEST PAGE

COLOR TEST PAGE

www.ingramcontent.com/pod-product-compliance
Lightning Source LLC
Chambersburg PA
CBHW081116280526
45787CB00007B/2850